Good Pets

By Mary Evans

Sadlier-Oxford
A Division of William H. Sadlier, Inc.

This dog is a good pet for me.

This hamster is a good pet for me.

This bird is a good pet for me.

This goldfish is a good pet for me.

This rabbit is a good pet for me.

This goat is a good pet for me.

And this kitten is a good pet for Koko.